JURISPRUDENCE(FIQH) OF MARRIAGE

ZEESHAN AIJAZ

Contents

BOOK TITLE

THE JURISPRUDENCE(FIQH)

OF MARRIAGE.

ZEESHAN AIJAZ.

TABLE OF CONTENTS.

9 PROHIBITION OF SPREADING BEDROOM SECRETS.

what is marriage

First Khutbah: Slaves of Allah! The more avenues are opened for evil, the harder we need to strive in opening gates for good; so, the more facilitated it becomes for people to sin, the more mandatory it is to make the means of attaining virtue possible. If one looks at lusts and desires nowadays, he would be astonished to the different ways used to move them and instigate them. The eyes of the pious are as though being cut by (obscene) pictures flashing everywhere, intermingling and chatting between men and women, ladies not adhering to Hijaab (Islaamically prescribed attire for women) in the presence of their relatives, in hospitals, offices, traveling, etc; it is these manifestations that have intensified the fire of desires and kindled its flame. People ask where they should go and what the cure is after their lust and passion have been stimulated, whilst the Jews and their allies continue to make every effort to increase the intensity of this fire even more. Allah wants to accept your repentance, but those who follow their passions want you to digress into a great deviation, and Allah wants to lighten for you your difficulties; and mankind was created weak. His weakness is due to surrendering to his desires and passions, which leads him to destruction.

Dear brothers! All praise is due to Allah, Who made Islaam a perfect and complete religion, in all aspects. There are certain deeds which act as preventive measures before anything evil happens. For example, lowering one's gaze is a precautionary step, as Allah says that which means: "Tell the believing men to lower their gaze (i.e., looking only at what is lawful and averting their eyes from what is unlawful.) ... And tell the believing women to reduce [some] of their vision ..." (An-Noor: 30-31).

Furthermore, a woman is attracted by men, even though men are more fascinated and affected by women; hence, the prohibition of men segregating with women is another example of a deterrent.

Beloved Muslims! Do you not think that the spreading of impermissible acts necessitates that we re-evaluate the issue of marriage and facilitate it? Corruption is approaching us from all directions, for it seems that what we had on the ground was not enough, that they (the disbelievers) have attacked us even from the skies (i.e., by means of satellites). They have disseminated evil everywhere, to the extent that teenagers are surely exposed to prohibitions through satellite channels and they may even watch pornography; they see naked or virtually nude women on television – what, then, is the solution?

Dear brothers! We must take solid steps towards easing lawful means in this regard. Let us address the subject of the reasonable and proper age for marriage, for instance. There is a lot of misconception amongst people regarding this matter, which has resulted from the propaganda of the West through their movies and articles in magazines and newspapers. Islaam does not forbid marrying off one's daughter at a young age and neither does it allow forcing her to get married. Another thing that must be noted is that there is nothing wrong for the woman to be older than the man marrying her.

What does Islaam instruct? The Prophet sallallaahu alayhi wa sallam said: "When someone whose religion and character you are satisfied with, asks for your daughter's hand in marriage, accede to his request. If you do not do so, there will be corruption and great evil on the earth." This is regarding the way to choose a man; as for the way to choose a woman, he sallallaahu alayhi wa sallam said: "Marry the one whose religious you will prosper". Indeed, this is how simple the wedding should be. There must be no complications due to age, because the Prophet sallallaahu alayhi wa sallam married Khadeejah, may Allaah be pleased with her, while she was fifteen years older than him, and married 'Aa'ishah, may Allah be pleased with her, while she was quite younger than him.

Religious compatibility and qualification is a very important concern, because a sinful person is not fit for a pious woman, as Allah says that which means: "Then is one who was a believer like one who was defiantly disobedient? They are not equal." (As-Sajdah: 18). Therefore, it does not reflect sincerity that a guardian marries his pious daughter or sister off to an immoral man, because he is simply not eligible, and also, for the reason that Islaam has appointed a guardian (for a girl) for the validity of the contract, so he may protect her and look after her best interest. Why didn't the Prophet sallallaahu alayhi wa sallam consider the man's wealth, car or house when he set the condition of accepting the man proposing for marriage? It is the responsibility of the guardian to investigate the situation of the man proposing for his daughter's hand in marriage, because many divorces result due to the fact that the guardian never inspected the man or asked about him before the wedding. It is true that perhaps he may have asked the man's friends at work or a relative regarding him, but they would naturally say nothing but good about him.

Many parents set the condition that the girl must finish her university studies before getting married, which might make them reach an undesired age for men who usually look for younger women. This is a bad habit which people have adopted due to television films and by inventing traditions and customs, for which Allah has not sent down permission.

Some convictions which women have delay their marriage and they remain unmarried, all of which has a bad effect on men and women. Due to the spread of corruption everywhere in the era we live in some scholars rule that if the woman can only read and write, then she is ready for marriage.

The present situation leaves no room for delay, stating (pointless) demands or hindering marriages. Allah has made the contract a very simple one. The father or the guardian of the girl says: "I give you my daughter so-and-so in marriage, according to the Book of Allah and the Sunnah of the Prophet sallallaahu alayhi wa sallam", and the man proposing says: "I accept (that)", in the presence of two witnesses and the marriage contract has been effected. It is a very simple and straightforward issue in Islaam, but people make it complex by laying down such conditions, which when they are traced back are found to be based mainly on people's talk and not on the words of Allah or His Messenger sallallaahu alayhi wa sallam.

People say, why do you do such and such? People say, Why do you set such conditions for marriage? People say ... People say. We are fed up with the concern of what people will say; we only want what Allah and His Messenger sallallaahu alayhi wa sallam state. We need to free ourselves from social pressures in order to rescue our young men and women.

When Islaam gives authority to the guardian to conduct the contract, it does not mean that he may delay her marriage and deny her marrying a qualified man, because that is forbidden. Islaam deems it great oppression for both the man proposing and the woman, to deprive them from wedding, without an Islaamically legitimate reason.

Second Khutbah: Slaves of Allah! You have observed how Islaam has facilitated marriage and the means to achieve it, and how Islaam has prevented postponing it. Therefore, we must correspond with the objectives which Islaam has come to accomplish... we must see what Allah wants, what are the objectives in order to fulfill them; if the objective is to facilitate marriage and its means, then we must facilitate it. Whoever tries to set hurdles for marriage, goes against the Islaamic objectives, which is a very serious matter.

On the other hand, when a condition has been agreed upon, it must be fulfilled, because the Prophet sallallaahu alayhi wa sallam said: "From among all the conditions which you have to fulfill, the conditions which make it legal for you to have sexual relations (i.e. the marriage contract) have the greatest right to be fulfilled." Hence, if the stipulation is allowed and not prohibited, one must realize it, especially if he has accepted it. In any case, I advise you to not set such conditions which might make life difficult later.

The man asking for someone's hand in marriage should educate himself about wedding beforehand and know its rulings; thus, he should be mature when he approaches the issue. Many young men go to see the woman with one thing in mind – how beautiful is she? He wonders if she resembles those whom he had seen on a magazine cover, for example. This is the result of not lowering one's gaze, for looking at prohibitions definitely affects people and changes the way they think.

The key to all this is to be content with what Allah has decreed for you; undoubtedly, everything has a solution in Islaam, but it requires knowledge, wisdom and struggling against people's wrong habits and traditions. It entails that we set a practical example for others by applying Islaamic measures (when marrying) and that we approach the issue with wisdom and reason, by choosing the most suitable spouse and the one farthest from causing problems.

No one would refuse to marry a woman who possesses both beauty and religiosity; in fact, people's desire to marry her becomes even greater. Moreover, if she possesses beauty and wealth, in addition to her devotion to Islaam, she becomes even more desired, but the first criterion must be her commitment to faith.

CHAPTER TWO

THE DOWER AND RELATED FIQH ISSUES

THE TYPES OF RIGHTS OF THE WIFE UPON HER HUSBAND:

The wife has specific rights upon her husband that are the result of a sound marriage contract. Some of the rights are material rights while others are non material.

from the material rights of the women is the dower (al-sadaaq) it is also called al mahr,al fareedhah,al hibaa,al taul.

the reason it is called al sadaaq is because one feels the husbands sincerity in wanting to marry that women.In laws before us, the guardians would recieve the dower.

THE LEXICAL MEANING OF AL SADAAQ (THE DOWER):

The sadaaq it is better known as sadaaq than sidaaq is an exchange. It is said that it is an honoring for the wife the plural is asdiqah for small plurals and suduq for larger numbers.

WHAT REQUIRES THE GIVING OF THE DOWER:

The term sadaaq or mahr applies to everything that is required to be paid due to a marriage contract, sexual intercourse or in the case of forced seperation, such as due to having the same breastfeeding mother or the witness taking back their statements.

TECHNICAL DEFINITION OF DOWER:

As a technical,legal term, the dower is defined as something given in exchange for marriage or something similar,be it required by the judge or by agreement among two parties.

THE WISDOM BEHIND INSTITUTING THE DOWER:

Islam has legislated the giving of the dower by the husband to the wife in order to make the woman's heart pleased and to honor her. It is her possession and none of her guardian or relatives share any part of it no one has any power over her concerning how she wishes to dispose of it,as long as she does so in a legally acceptable manner she may give it away as a gift, she may lend it to others or she may give it in charity or do any other permissible acts she wishes with it.

THE RULING CONCERNING STATING THE DOWER AT THE TIME OF THE MARRIAGE CONTRACT:

It is sunnah to state the dower at the time of the marriage contract in order to prevent any future dispute or argumentation.This is based on allah's statement,

"All others [women other than those stated in the verse] are lawful for you provided you seek them [with a dower] from your wealth (al-nisa:24) and the messenger of allah said to the one who was to marry the women who had offered herself to the messenger of allah(peace be upon him),

"seek something even if it be a ring made of silver"

the scholars are agreed that it is sanctioned to state the dower at that time but it is not a prerequisite for the validity of the contract.

THE STATUS OF THE DOWER:

The dower is not a prerequisite or an essential component of the marriage contract.Instead it is one of its rulings and a requirement of a sound marriage.Therefore,a small amount of uncertainity concerning it is overlooked as well as a small amount of potential harm that is expected to be removed.This is because the goal of marriage is bringing the two together and having the two enjoy each other.If the marriage contract is concluded without the mentioning of a specific dower,the marriage contract is still valid.In that case,the husband is required to give his wife a dower which is comparable to the dower that women who are similar to his wife receive,according to the agreement of the scholars.

the evidence for this position is in allah's statement,

There is no sin upon you if you divorce women while you had not yet had sexual relations with them,nor appointed for them a dower (al-baqara 236).This verse permits divorce before consummation and before determining the dower.This indicates that the dower is neither a necessary component for the marriage contract.

In zaad al maseer, ibn al-jauzi stated, The verse indicates that it is allowed to have a marriage without stating a dower.

It is confirmed in the sunnah from uqbah ibn aamir who narrated that the prophet(peace be upon him) said to a man,would you be pleased if i were to marry you to so and so?he said, yes.Then he said to the woman would you be pleased if i were to marry you to so and so? she said, yes.So he married the two of them together.Uqbah consummated the marriage and did not establish any dower for her.When he was about to die he said the prophet(peace be upon him) married me to so and so and he did not establish any dower for her and i did not give her anything.Therefore i give her as a dower my share in khaibar.She took it and sold for two hundred thousand dinars.Based on that if two spouses agree to get married without a dower,the marriage is still valid according to the majority of the scholars(jumhoor)save the malikis.When the marriage is consummated or when the man dies,she has right to a dower that is comparable to the dower given to those women who are similar to her.According to the malikis (imam maalik) if two agree to get married without a dower,the marriage is not valid.

[zaad al maseer vol 1
   al fiqh al islami vol 7
   kashaaf al-qina vol 5

CONCLUSION:

To state the dower at the time of marriage contract is not essential component nor a condition for the validity of the marriage contract.This is because the dower is a resultant ruling that follows from the contract and it is not necessary to mention the ruling that are the result of the contract when the *contract is actually being stated.This is also based on the previous evidence given.In al-mughni it states,marriage is sound without stating of the dower according to vast majority of scholars(jumhoor).*

However,ibn taymmiyah has concluded that one should state dower at the time of marriage contract in order to avoid any dispute.He also concluded that the dower is essential component of marriage and dower must be mentioned or she is to be given what is given to women similar to her.

He wrote, Those who state that the dower is not a goal in itself are making a statement that has no truth to it.It is,in fact an essential component of marriage and it being a condition of it makes it more important than the price prophet (peace be upon him) said,the conditions that have the most right to be fulfilled are those conditions that makes the private parts lawful.Wealth is permissible in exchange for other wealth.However,the private parts are not permissible for another except with the dower.A marriage can be enacted without stating or fixing the amount of dower but it cannot be enacted while negating the dower.For the marriage in which the dower is not stated, the dower then becomes the dower of a similar woman.

Therefore there are three possible scenarios:

one case is where the two agree upon not having a dower.This is not allowed and such a marriage contract is not valid.

second case is where the dower is clearly stated at the time of marriage contract this is normal and most complete case

Third case is where the dower is not mentioned at the time of marriage contract.This is permissible and the women will then receive what women similar to her receive or whatever they may later agree upon.

[recorded by al-bukhari 5151

muslim 1418

majmoo fatawa ibn taymmiyah vol 29 p 344]

THE MAXIMUM AMOUNT OF DOWER ALLOWED:

The jurists (fuqaha) agree that there is no maximum limit to the dower,since there is nothing stated in the shareeah mentioning an upper limit.Allah says in the quran

But if you intend to replace a wife by another and you have given one a qintaar(large amount of gold),take not the least bit back of it, would you take it wrongfully without a right and in manifest sin?(AL-NISA 20).

The mention of qintaar is not meant to place an upper limit to the dower but it is simply a figurative expression implying a great amount.If that were meant to state the greater limit to the dower,allah would have prohibited us from going beyond that.

THE MINIMUM AMOUNT ALLOWABLE FOR A DOWER:

Concerning the minimum amount permissible for a dower,there are five well known opinions.

The jurists (scholars of fiqh) have stated the maximum and minimum allowed dower in terms of dirhams and dinars because they were the monetary units common among the people in the past.Therefore it would be good to discuss their origins and their weights in modern terms.Dirham is a greek word drachma,and it is a word for a silver coin that is equivalent to seven tenths of a dinar therefore in order to know the weight of dirham one must know the weight of a dinar.Dinar comes from latin greek term dinariyus and it was one of the most important coins used in the islamic lands.Its weight in grams is 4.25grams.Since a dirham is seven tenths of that its weight is 2.975 grams.

The first opinion is that a proper dower cannot be less than ten dirhams. This is the opinion of the fiqh hanafi(IMAM ABU HANIFA).

The second opinion is that the minimum acceptable for a dower is three dirhams, a quarter of a dinar or what is equivalent in value to that of goods or of something pure and not impure, something that is considered wealth, assests or property from a shareeah perspective, this is the opinion of fiqh maliki(imam maalik).

A third opinion is that the dower is valid as long as anything which can be called wealth or its equivalent is given, as long as the parties mutually consent to it. This is the opinion of shafi'ees(imam shafi'ee) and hanbalis(imam ahmad), ibn wahb of malikis, ishaaq ibn rahawaih, abu thaur, the jurists of the madinah at the time of the followers al-hasan-al-busri, ul-uuzuu'ee, saeed ibn al-musayyab.

A fourth opinion is that anything which may be called a thing, even if it is just a grain of barley, is acceptable as the dower. This was the opinion of ibn hazm.

A fifth opinion is that the dower is valid by anything which has value,either material or non material.

THE EVIDENCE:

Those of the first opinion,that the minimum dower is ten dirhams,support their view with following evidence:

First is what is recorded by al-daaraqutni and al-baihaqi from jaabir ibn abdullah that the prophet(peace be upon him) said,no one is to marry women off except the guardians.They are not to be married except to those who are suitable.There is no dower less than ten dirhams.

This hadith has been objected to because it is weak.Therefore, it is not proper to use it as evidence.It was narrated by mubashir ibn ubaid.

Second is what is recorded by al-baihaqi through the chain of shuraik on the authority of dawood al-audee on the authority of al-shaabi on the authority of hazrat ali who said,the minimum that makes the private parts of wife permissible is ten dirhams.

Their third argument is that the amount must be something that reflects the greatness of making private parts allowable.Just any amount of wealth would not meet that requirement.The shareeah has stated the amount by which a part of the human may be taken and that is ten dirhams,as in the case of prescribed punishment for the thief and it is that amount that must be paid to make the private parts legal.

This argument is refuted because the amount for which the hand of a thief is cut off has no relevance here.Marriage is sought for pleasure and love while cutting off the hand of thief is a type of punishment.Furthermore,why did they determine the amount of dower according to what requires the hand to be cut off instead of the amount that prophet(peace be upon him) gave his wives as a dower or minimum amount due to which one must pay zakat,which is two hundred dirhams or twenty dinars.

The people of the second opinion support their view by the quran and sunnah from the quran,they quote the verse,And whoever among you has not the means (taul) to wed free believing women,they may wed believing women from among those whom your right hand possess(al-nisa 25).The argument from the verse is that allah has laid down the condition of lack of means in order for one to marry a slave girl,because not everyone possesses the means(which is stated as taul in verse).The meaning of taul here is wealth.The word wealth is not applied to less than three dirhams.Therefore what is less than three dirhams does not qualify for a marriage.

This argument is criticized because the meaning of taul in that verse is not just wealth.Its meaning is wider than that,it also refers to virtuosness and ability in both spiritual and material sense.A man could have plenty of wealth, more than what is needed for a customary dower of a free women,but women flee from him due to a shortcoming in his physical being or character and therefore he is not able to marry a free woman.Furthermore,he may not be able to fulfill the rights of a free woman other than dower.Free woman have many rights,such as maintenance,equality in multiple marriages and so forth.The slave does not have all of those right.Therefore lacking taul can actually manifest itself in many different ways.

Their evidence from the sunnah is what is narrated from hazrat anas that the prophet (peace be upon him) saw abdul rahman ibn auf wearing dyed clothing.He asked him,what is this? he answered ,i married a woman with a nawaah amount of gold as a dower , the prophet(peace be upon him) told him,may allah bless you.Give a dinner party even if with just a sheep.

They say that nawaah among the people of madinah was equivalent to one quarter of dinar.

However, the argument based on this hadith is objected to because there is no evidence that what is stated in the hadith,one quarter of a dinar is the minimum for a dower.Just because there was a dower of that amount does not negate the possibility that less is permissible unless there is a clear statement indicating that less than that is not sufficient but there is no such statement here.

The people of the third opinion the shafi'ees and hanbalis,say that anything that is wealth or that can take place of wealth is permissible as a dower.They use the quran and sunnah to support their view.From the quran,the quote the verse that states after declaring which woman a man cannot marry.

And permissible for you is anyone other than those,as long as you seek them by your wealth(al-nisa 24).The argument here is that the word wealth is stated in an unconditional sense and inclusive of both a small amount of wealth or a great deal of wealth.

The objection to this argument is that the quranic expression indicates that what is not AMWAAL is not acceptable as a dower.Therefore,the condition is that the dower must be AMWAAL.This is the necessary and apparent meaning of the verse.Anyone who has just one or two dirhams cannot be called someone who has AMWAAL.Therefore,the necessary and apparent meaning of the verse is that the one or two dirhams is not acceptable as a dower.

From the sunnah,they use the hadith

Whoever makes the private parts permissible by a dirham has made them permissible in a legal way.Al-haithami said about the chain of narrators for this hadith,it contains yahya ibn abdul rahmaan ibn abi kabshah who is weak.This argument has also been objected to by noting that there is no proof in this evidence as it is a report about having the right to the private parts and does not indicate that nothing else is obligatory.

[AL-mughni vol 8
    ahkaam al quraan vol 2 p 170
    majma al zawaaid wa manba al-fawaaid vol 4]

One more evidence is what is recorded by abu dawood and al-tirmidhi on the authority of aamir ibn rabeeah that a women from tribe of fazaarah married with a dower of a pair of shoes.The prophet(peace be upon him) asked her is your soul and wealth content with a pair of shoes? she said, yes, so he permitted it.

This proof is objected to because it is weak hadith.

Another opinion is that the dower is valid as long as it is something of value,either material or non material.This is the opinion with strongest evidence.It is also consistent with the proper shareeah meaning of the dower,in that the purpose of the dower is not simply an exchange of the wealth.Instead it is meant to be a token of man's wanting that woman and the sincerity of his intention in coming together with her.This is usually conveyed by giving some type of wealth.However,it may be with anything that has value as long as the wife agrees to it.

If a woman is pleased to accept the knowledge of her husband that he will impart to her and what he has memorized quran as her dower,this is permissible.If she is pleased to accept a person's knowledge,embracing of islam or his reading of the quran such a dower is from the most beneficial types of dower.

EXTRAVAGANT DOWERS: THE CAUSES,RESULTS AND RULING:

PRELIMINARY DISCOURSE:

The dower is an obligatory right for the woman.The shareeah has made it an obligation as a token of the man's interest in the woman.It is one of the signs of love and a bond of compassion and mercy.It is an unavoidable obligation concerning which the man has no option but to give it.It is given as a sign of respect for his betrothed and a gesture to her honor,preciousness and esteem.Allah says in the quran,

And give the women their dowers graciously.But if they remit a portion willingly,then take it in satisfaction and ease(al-nisa 4).

This does not mean that a woman is a piece of merchandise to be bought or sold.Instead,the dower is a token for her honor and esteem.It takes into consideration the woman's natural desires for items of pleasure and her eagerness for adornments.Furthermore,the giving of wealth indicates the husband's intent upon fulfilling his responsibilities and attending to her rights.

Islam awoke the people to consider the dower as a token and not as a price for the woman.Islam also exhorted the people not to be extravagant with respect to the dower and go beyond the proper limits since,after all,the dower is not actually a goal in itself.

The prophet(peace be upon him) was the excellent example.On this particular issue,he established for the muslim nation a splendid practice,so that the reality of the matter would be well established in the sincere and thoughtful society and that the spirit of ease and simplicity would be well known among the people.His(peace be upon him) simplicity when it came to the dower of his daughters is an indication that he wanted to spread that understanding among the people.Ibn Abbas narrated that when hazrat ali married fatimah,the prophet(peace be upon him) told Ali,give her something.He replied i do not have anything.The prophet(peace be upon him) said, where is your smashed armor plate? he said,i have it.So the prophet(peace be upon him) said,give it to her.

This confirms that the dower,from an islamic perspective,is not the goal in and of itself.It is also not setting a price for the worth of the woman.In fact,it is sanctioned to be easy in setting dowers and not to be extravagant.A hadith states,

The best dower is the easiest for the person to meet.The prophet(peace be upon him) also said,

From the blessings related to a woman are the facilitating of her proposal,the facilitating of her dower and the facilitating of her womb.

The wisdom behind forbidding extravagant dower is obvious.It is to make marriages easier upon the people,so that they do not become adverse to it and therefore succumb to various evil social ills and practices.

Definitely,the dower is simply a token and not a price for merchandise.Furthermore,the happiness of a household is not found in extravagant,waste and burdening when it comes to the dower AL-TIRMIDHI recorded and declared authentic the narration from AAMIR IBN RABEEAH that a woman from the tribe of fazaarah married and the dower was a pair of shoes.The prophet(peace be upon him) asked her,is your soul and wealth pleased with a pair of shoes? she replied yes, and therefore the prophet(peace be upon him) allowed the marriage.

[RECORDED BY AHMAD IN AL-MUSNAD VOL 6].

Ibn al-qayyim stated,after mentioning a number of hadith in which the prophet(peace be upon him) issued some decrees concerning the dower.

These hadith imply that there is no minimum established amount for the dower.A handful of flour,a pair of shoes can all validly be declared the dower and by them the marriage is valid.These hadith also imply that it is disapproved to have extravagant dowers for the marriage and such reduces its blessings and makes it more difficult.

There is no room in islam for that materialistic approach that has overcome the thoughts of many people who,therefore,demand exorbitant dowers.The sitiuation has deteriorated to such an extent that hardly any people leave a marriage ceremony without discussing how much the dower was.It is as if they were leaving from an auction.A woman is not a piece of merchandise that is sold in some kind of woman's market such that people should be speaking about her in such a purely materialistic fashion.

ABU AL-UJAFAA AL-SULAMI said that he heard umar ibn al-khattab say,

do not become exorbitant when it comes to the dowers of woman.Verily,if such a thing were noble in this world or act of obedience to allah,the first one to demand such would be the prophet(peace be upon him).However,he never gave in dower to his wives or asked for dower for his daughters anything in excess of twelve auqiyah.A man goes to such an extreme in getting a dower for his wife that there develops an enmity for her in him,and he says i burdened myself the rope of the waterskin for you.

The maliki jurist ibn al arabi stated, an auqiyah according to the people of knowledge equals forty dirhams so twelve auqiyah equals four hundred and eighty dirhams.

Exorbitant   dowers,extravagance pomp,ignorant customs,wrongful taking of a woman's dower and using it for purposeless show are the causes behind many young men not being able to marry and many women becoming old maids nowadays.If only people would follow the islamic path when it comes to values,not allowing evil customs to distance them from what is proper nor having evil practices take sway over them,the structure and health of the household would not be in the state of disrepair that we witness today.

The houses have become filled with old maids due to the numerous conditions that the people place on the men proposing and the heavy burdens that they must face.These conditions sometimes come from the woman herself or her guardian or are due to the prevalent customs and norms of her tribe.

[recorded by abu dawood 2106 the book of marriage
ahmad al musnad 285,286.
sunan al nasaai vol 6]

IBN TAYMIYAH wrote,

only a fool could lead himself to requiring a dower for his daughters that is larger than the dower of the daughters of the prophet(peace be upon him).As for the poor person he must not agree to a dower that he is not able to pay without undergoing hardship.

THE CAUSES BEHIND EXORBITANT DOWERS

1:The abundance of wealth is a major cause.This phenomenon did not exist until the people had abundant wealth and their pockets became filled.The strong winds of this new modern day rich society then brought about many new things that were not existent before.

2:The desire of the husband to show that he is rich and well to do and his desire to convince his wife and her guardians that he is well to do.

3:Blind following others if other person did something,then the next in line must also do the same otherwise he will be considered cheap and will be exposed to insults from the people.

4:Allowing women to decide and get involved in these matters.listening to their opinions and fulfilling their wants,not distinguishing between what is a sound demand and what is not.

THE NEGATIVE CONSEQUENCES OF EXORBITANT DOWERS.

1:Most of the young men have to remain bachelors and most of the young women become old maids.The young man who has little or no wealth will soon become depressed and sad.

2:Immorality spreads between the two sexes when they have no means to marry and they seek a substitute for its pleasure.

3:psychological problems afflict the young men and women due to supression of their natural needs and crushing of their dreams and aspirations.

THE RULING CONCERNING EXORBITANT DOWERS.

Among the scholars there are three opinions on this issue.

1:exorbitant dowers are allowed.

2:exorbitant dowers are not allowed.

3:different cases need to be discussed separately.

THE FIRST OPINION:The first opinion states that exorbitant dowers are permissible.An evidence for this view is the following verse of quran.

If you have given one of them a great amount(qintaar) do not take any of it back (AL NISA 20).While commenting on this verse ibn katheer stated,in this verse there is an indication that it is alowed to give u great deal of wealth as a dower.

The dower according to the shareeah is a gift and offering thus it has no prescribed limit.People differ with respect to being rich or poor,so the shareeah has left everyone to set its limit according to their ability.

THE SECOND OPINION:The second opinion is that it is not allowed to have exorbitant dowers.the followers of this view reply to the verse that was used as evidence by people of first opinion by saying that the verse is irrelevant to this issue by following reason.

First example of a qintaar is only an exaggerated method to stress the point that even if one had given them a great deal of wealth he cannot take back any portion of it.It is similar in vein to the prophet's (peace be upon him) statement,

For whoever builds a mosque for the sake of allah the size of a grouse's nest allah will build for him a house in paradise but there cannot be a mosque the size of grouse's nest.

WHEN THE WOMAN IS ENTITLED TO HER ENTIRE DOWER.

The jurists agree that it is certain that the entire dower must be paid to the woman as a result of a sound marriage that has been consummated or in which the husband has died.This is true regardless of whether the amount of the dower was explicitly stated or if it were a dower that was unstated and the same as woman who are similar to the wife.None of the obligation of paying the entire dower is to be dropped unless it was already paid or if the one who has the right to it gives it up of her own accord.

According to the strongest opinions among the scholars the woman is entitled to her entire dower as a result of a complete seclusion with her husband after a valid marriage.According to fiqh maliki the woman is entitled to her complete dower if she spends one year in the house of her husband even if they did not have sexual intercourse.According to fiqh hanbali she is also entitled to her entire dower if the husband is on his deathbed and divorces her only to prevent her from inheriting from him,even if such is done before consummation.Imam Ahmad specifically stated that any kind of physical pleasure such as kissing with wife,even if it less than sexual intercourse and not in private requires that the woman receive her entire dower.

THE DEATH OF EITHER SPOUSE AFTER A SOUND MARRIAGE AND EVEN BEFORE CONSUMMATION ACCORDING TO AGREEMENT OF SCHOLARS.

If either spouse dies after a sound marriage yet before consummation the woman is entitled to her entire dower.This is because the marriage contract is not annuled by the death.The contract simply comes to an end due to the death of one of the parties.

According to fiqh maliki,if the dower was not explicitly stated in the contract,the woman is not entitled to anything.They make an analogy between this case and the cases of death while divorced,divorce from consummation or private seclusion and before stating the dower.

According to majority of jurists in such case she is entitled to receive the same dower of woman who are similar to her.

THE WIFE STAYING ONE YEAR IN THE HOUSE OF THE HUSBAND.

According to fiqh maliki if wife stays in house of her husband for one year and he does not have sexual intercourse with her,she is still entitled to her entire dower.However fiqh hanafi,fiqh shafiee,and fiqh hanbali disagree with this opinion.

PAYING HALF OF THE DOWER.

Jurists agreed that the wife has a right to only half of her agreed upon dower that was part of sound marriage contract,if the husband divorces her before consummating the marriage or before being in complete privacy with her.This is based on the verse

if you divorce them before touching them and you have determined their dowers then they shall receive half of the dowers(AL BAQARA 237).

THE QUESTION OF BEING ALONE WITH ONE'S FIANCEE BEFORE THE ACTUAL CONTRACTING OF THE MARRIAGE.

This practice of the man being alone with his betrothed,so that they may experience and know each other as a means leading to love between them,is an evil practice that exists in many muslim lands.

This distasteful custom has slowly crept over muslim society and has now become a blind custom that people follow and that is supported by the evildoers.

In their ignorance of the laws of islam they claim and they are completely wrong that when the two are engaged and on the road to getting married,then the things are permissible under marriage become permissible for them.

CASES WHEREIN THE MAN IS NOT OBLIGED TO PAY ANY PORTION OF THE DOWER.

There are four cases:

1:Any type of seperation,other than divorce before consummation or complete privacy means that the man does not have to pay any portion of the dower.This is the case whether the seperation was from the wife's side or from husband's side.

The fiqh maliki say that if the husband annuls the marriage or returns the wife due to some problem with her before consummation then he is not obliged to pay any portion of dower.

2:IN THE CASE OF KHULA,EITHER BEFORE OR AFTER CONSUMMATION WHEREIN THE WIFE AGREES TO RETURN HER DOWER.

If the two are seperated through khula wherein they agree that the woman will return her entire dower,then the obligation to pay the dower is dropped.If the dower was one that the woman had not previously taken possession of,then the husband is freed from responsibility to now pay it.

3:WHEN THE WIFE FREES THE HUSBAND OF THE OBLIGATION OF THE DOWER,EITHER BEFORE OR AFTER CONSUMMATION.

If the wife is from those people who can donate wealth and the dower is one that the husband has to pay in the future,such as money or specific weight or amount of some item and not something specific that was a purpose in itself she is allowed to free him from that obligation.

4:WHEN THE WIFE GIVES THE ENTIRE DOWER AS A GIFT TO THE HUSBAND.

When the woman is qualified to give gifts or donations and the husband agrees to accept the dower as a gift,she may return entire dower to the husband regardless of whether that was before she took possession of the dower or afterwards.

THE RULING CONCERNING PAYING THE DOWER ON SPOT OR OVER TIME.

It is proper for the dower to be paid either promptly or over time.It is also proper if part of it is paid promptly and the reminder is to be paid at a later time.This is because it is a type of transaction and therefore it is allowed to be delayed

The jurists state that it is acceptable to pay the dower at a later time if such is agreed upon.

ENGAGEMENT RINGS: THEIR RULING FOR MEN OR WOMEN.

An engagement ring is often one of those gifts that the fiance gives to fiancee before marriage contract.This is newly adopted custom and an objectionable innovation.

The jurists are agreed that it is permissible for the women to wear a gold ring and that such is forbidden for men.ABU HURAIRAH reported that the prophet(peace be upon him) prohibited gold rings for men.

[recorded by al bukhari 5864 the book of dress].

CHAPTER THREE

ANNOUNCING THE MARRIAGE.

THE RULING CONCERNING MAKING THE MARRIAGE KNOWN.

The majority of the scholars say that making the marriage known publicly is a recommended act.

AL ZUHRI was of the opinion that the announcing of the marriage is obligatory.In fact,he said that if a secret marriage is contracted and two male witnesses were present but those witnesses were ordered to keep the marriage secret,then one must seperate the man and woman.The woman is then to enter her waiting period and she is to receive her dower.If they insist on getting married before her waiting period is over,they may remarry but they must publicly announce the marriage.

THE MEANING OF ANNOUNCING THE MARRIAGE.

To announce the marriage is to publicize it and spread the news about it.

one of the means of publicizing the wedding is by beating the duff(handdrum).The duff is a musical instrument that is played it is also called al kirbaal.It does not have any bangles or rings.if it contains such bangles or rings it is called mizhar.

As for the poetry that is accompanied by musical instruments that mentions the attributes of women or erotic songs that spread evil and lewdness among young men and women and destroys the values and changes their ways there is no doubt such are forbidden according to the agreement of compainions,followers and four imams,IMAM ABU HANIFA,IMAM SHAFIEE,IMAM MAALIK,IMAM AHMAD may allah be pleased with them.

DANCING.

Dancing is the movement and shifting of the body according to a musical rhythm or otherwise.

Dancing is one of the greatest forms of error and going astray by which many of the dreams and desires of the enimies of islaam are fulfilled among the muslims.

THE CEREMONY OF PRESENTING THE BRIDE AND GROOM.

This practice has no source in the quraan or sunnah neither the prophet(peace be upon him) nor companions or early scholars ever did anything of this nature.If it were something good they would have done it.The groom enters upon a number of women and they are not wearing the proper islamic attire hijaab.

CHAPTER FOUR

THE WEDDING DINNER(AL-WALEEMAH) AND AN ADMONITION CONCERNING EXTRAVAGANCE AT WEDDING PARTIES.

THE ROOT OF THE WORD WALEEMAH.

The root of the word waleemah is completing something and gathering it together.ibn arabi said,

It is said that a man has awalam when his intelligence and character come together.The one who is shackled is called walm because one of his legs is tied to the other.

THE RULING OF CONCERNING WALEEMAH.

The wedding feast waleemah is a strongly recommended sunnah according to the majority of scholars.

ABU HURAIRAH narrates that the prophet(peace be upon him) said,

The wedding feast is a right act haqq and sunnah one who is invited to it but does not attend has disobeyed.

THE AMOUNT OF THE WALEEMAH AND WHAT IT CONSISTS OF.

Based on what the prophet(peace be upon him)said to abdul rahman ibn auf,give a wedding feast even if it just be a sheep.The scholars sat that it is preffered for one who has the means to offer a feast of no less than a sheep.However it is confirmed that the prophet(peace be upon him)himself had a wedding feast for one of his wives with something less than a sheep.

THE INVITATION TO ATTEND THE WALEEMAH.

It is the practice in islam for husband to feed his family,companions,neighbours during the waleemah.He should also set aside a portion for the poor as a way of expressing thanks to allah.

CHAPTER FIVE

THE RIGHTS OF SPOUSES.

THE RIGHTS OF THE HUSBAND UPON HIS WIFE.

The foundation upon which the husband's rights over his wife are based in the verse of quran,

Men are in charge of woman by right of what qualities allah has given one over the other and what they spend from their wealth so righteous woman are obedient guarding in absense what allah would have them guard.But those from whom you fear defiance,admonish them forsake them in their beds and strike them but if they obey you seek no means against them(al-nisa 34).

The most obvious of the rights of the husband upon his wife are the following:

OBEDIENCE.

The evidence for this is in what husain ibn muhsin narrated:my aunt narrated to me that she said,i came to the prophet(peace be upon him)and he said are you married?she said yes,he said,how are you with respect to him? she said,i do not fail him in a anything except for what i am not able to do,he said,see how you are with respect to himfor he is your paradise or your hell fire.

REMAINING IN THE HOUSE AND NOT GOING OUT EXCEPT WITH THE HUSBAND'S PERMISSION.

Allah says in the quran,

And stay in your houses and do not display yourselves like that during the times of ignorance(al-ahzaab 33) in this verse allah ordered the wives of prophet and the women of this nation also follow them in this order,to remain in their houses as a protection for them and a way of guarding the rights of husband.

NOT ALLOWING ANYONE TO ENTER HIS HOUSE EXCEPT WITH HIS PERMISSION.

It is not permissible for the wife to allow someone to enter her husband's house if that is displeasing to the husband.The prophet(peace be upon him) said,

and your right upon them is that they do not allow anyone whom you dislike to sit on your cushion.

SERVING THE HUSBAND.

From the rights of husband upon the wife is that she must serve him in such matters as bringing up the children,preparing his food,taking care of his clothes and so forth.

PROTECTING HIS HONOR,CHILDREN AND WEALTH.

The wife must protect her chastity and be careful about and avoid anything that might strain his honor and reputation.

THE RIGHTS OF WIFE,

The wife also has rights over her husband some are financial while others are not financial.

TREATING THE WIFE IN A KIND AND GOOD MANNER.

Treating in a kind and good manner implies accompanying them in a good way,not delaying in fulfilling their rights when onc has the ability to fulfill them and demonstrating pleasure and happiness with them.The basis for this is in the statement of allah,

And treat them in good and kind manner(al-nisa19).Allah also says,

And they have rights similar to those over them according to what is reasonable(al-baqara 228).

TEACHING HER THE MATTERS OF RELIGION AND SUPPORTING HER IN ACTS OF OBEDIENCE TO ALLAH

Allah says in the quran,

O you who have believed protect yourself and your families from a fire whose fuel is people and stones(al-tahreem 6).

FINANCIALLY MAINTAINING THE WIFE.

Maintaining the wife is a necessary right of the wife.it is inclusive of food,clothing,and housing according to the situation of husband and what is within his means.Allah has made it obligatory.

CHAPTER SIX

LESSONS FOR HAPPY MARRIAGE.

THE RIGHT TO SLEEP AND LIVE IN PEACE.

This may sound obvious,but there are those who either overlook this point or ignore it.There are many men who come home late at night after having a fun time with their friends, and expect their wives to fulfil their desires immediately.They believe or at least their action suggests they believe that the wife is merely a servant who cooks,cleans,looks after the children and presents herself for their enjoyment when they so desire.Men have been prevented from engaging in voluntary forms of worship to ensure that they do not ignore the psychological and emotional needs of the wife.Having a fun time with one's friend may become a sinful act.

EDUCATION.

Perhaps this is sometimes even more necessary for the husband to do than providing his wife with food and clothing.Especially when she has not had any islamic orientation.

THE RIGHT TO BE KEPT IN HONOUR AND DIGNITY.

This is one of the most prominent rights of the wife over her husband.The husband should do everything to protect his wife's honour and dignity particularly in front of other people.

THE RIGHTS OF BOTH HUSBAND AND WIFE OVER EACH OTHER.

The third type of right is common between couple.

NOT TO REVEAL SECRETS.

This is a general rule for both parties and both will be held equally responsible to uphold the other's confidentiality.The prophet(peace be upon him) said,the man who will be the most wretched in status,in the eyes of allah on the day of judgement,will be the husband who confides in his wife and she in him,and then he goes and reveals her secret.

MUTUAL ADVICE.

This plays a very big role in the development of marriage and household in general.spouses should advise one another and even take account of and check each other.

TRUE LOVE BETWEEN THE COUPLE.

Marriage cannot be successful without this.Each spouse should at least express love towards the other.Prophet(peace be upon him) used to offer words of love and affection towards his wives.

BEING REALISTIC IN EXPECTATIONS AND AVOIDING FANTASIES.

Very few people live up to this reality.Many couples paint a fantastic picture in their minds before marriage and assume their spouses to be something very similar to the spouses of paradise.

A REALISTIC APPROACH IN ASKING FOR RIGHTS AND FULFILMENT OF RESPONSIBILITIES.

Although the husband and wife both have rights,it is not proper that they violate each other's rights and demand unrealistic chores from each other.

UNDERSTANDING THE SPOUSE'S PSYCHOLOGICAL FRAME OF MIND.

This is necessary for the compatibility of marriage.But despite this,many couples do not bother to give this issue any attention.This involves the likes and dislikes of each other and what pleases and displeases each other.

BEARING A CHILD.

Many husbands ask their wives to use contraceptive devices after marriage because they want to enjoy them first.

RAISING THE CHILDREN.

People have different ideas and methods about how to raise and educate their children.If there are disputes should be settled in private and not in front of children.

ADJUSTMENTS.

This means that both spouses adapt and adjust themselves to the nature of the other.

RESTRAINING THE TONGUE.

One of the best ways for a person to avoid fights and disputes.

NOT TO TAKE DISPUTES OUTSIDE THE HOUSE.

Trying to resolve problems by taking matters to others,especially to the family of spouse,is giving fuel to fire.This is because others do not know all the aspects and angles of problems and will become biased arbiters.Arguments are usually preceded by minor or silly comments made by spouse.

THE WIFE'S WEALTH AND PROPERTY.

Some men become greedy when they see that his wife has money.They force her to part with it.This is unlawful in islam,the wife has absolute control and authority over her wealth.

DRESSING UP.

Beauty plays a great role in creating a happy marriage.Man by nature,is lured towards beauty.

GIFTS.

Perhaps the best issue to discuss at the end of this lecture is the issue of offering gifts to one another.Many fail to realise that this has a great impact on marriage.This also applies to giving gifts to each other's parents.

CHAPTER SEVEN

KINDNESS TOWARDS WIFE.

SHOWING KINDNESS TOWARDS WIFE.

It is desirable, when one goes into his wife on his wedding night, to show her kindness, such as presenting her with something to drink, etc. This is found in the hadith narrated by Asmaa' bint Yazid ibn As-Sakan who said: "I beautified 'As'ishah for Allaah's Messenger, then called him to come to see her unveiled. He came, sat next to her, and brought a large cup of milk from which he drank. Then, he offered it to 'Aa'ishah, but she lowered her head and felt shy. I scolded her and said to her: "Take from the hand of the Prophet." She then took it and drank some. Then, the Prophet said to her, "Give some to your companion." At that point, I said: "O Messenger of Allaah, rather take it yourself and drink, and then give it to me from your hand." He took it, drank some, and then offered it to me. I sat down and put it on my kness. Then, I began rotating it andfollowing it with my lips in order that I might hit the spot from which the Prophet had drunk. Then, the Prophet said about some women who were there with me: "Give them some." But, they said: " don't want it." (ie. we are not hungry). The Prophet said:We "Do not combine hunger and fibbing!" [Ahmad and al-Humaidi. Ahmad reports it with 2 isnaads - one of which supports the other, and it is supported...]"

PLACING YOUR HANDS ON YOUR WIFE'S HEAD AND PRAYING FOR HER.

The husband should, at the time of consummating the marriage with his wife or before that, place his hand on the front part of her head, mention the name of Allah Most High, and pray for Allah's blessings. As in the statement of the Prophet: "When any of you marries a woman ... he should hold her forelock, mention Allah Most High, and pray for His blessings saying:

"O Allah, I ask You for the good in her and the good with which You have created her, and I seek refuge in You from the evil in her and the evil with which You have created her. [Aboo Dawood and others. Al-Bukhari in "Af'aalul -'Ibaad", Abu Dawood, Ibn Majah, al-Haakim, al- Baihaqee and Abu Ya'laa with hasan isnaad ...]

THE PRAYING OF HUSBAND AND WIFE TOGETHER.

It is desirable for the husband and wife to pray 2 rakaat together on their wedding night.This has been narrated from the earliest generation of Muslims, as in the following 2 Narrations: First: On the authority of Abu Sa'eed Mawla Abu Asyad who said: "I got married while I was a slave. I invited a number of the companions of the Prophet, among them was Ibn Mas'ood, Abu Dharr and Hudhaifa. When the prayer was called, Abu Dharr began to step forward when the others said to him: 'No!' He said: 'Is it so?' And they said: 'Yes.' Then, I stepped forward and led the prayer though I was a slave possessed. They taught me, saying: 'When your wife comes to you, pray 2 rakaat. Then, ask Allah for the good of that which has come to you, and seek refuge in Him from its evil. Then it is up to you and it is up to your wife.'" [Ibn Abi Shaibah and 'Abdur-Razzaaq] Second: On the authority of Shaqeeq who said: "A man named Abu Hareez came and said: 'I have married a young girl, and I am afraid that she will despise me.' 'Abdullah ibn Mas'ood said to him: "Verily, closeness is fromAllah, and hatred is from Shaitaan, who wishes to make despicable that which Allah has allowed. So, when your wife comes to you, tell her to pray behind you 2 rakaat.'" In another version of the same story, "'Abdullah went on to say: 'And say: 'O Allah give Your blessings on me in my wife, and to her in me. O Allah join us together as long as You join us in good, and split us apart if You send to us that which is better.'" [Ibn Abi Shaibah and at-Tabaraani and 'Abdur-Razzaaq: Saheeh].

WHAT TO SAY AT THE TIME OF MAKING LOVE.

When a Muslim man is about to enter his wife, he should always say first: [In the name of Allah, O Allah, keep us away from the devil, and keep the devil away from that which You may grant us (ie. offspring).] About this, the Prophet said: "After that, if Allah decrees that they will have a child, the devil will never be able to harm that child". [al-Bukhari] [Some Scholars say that children are disobedient to their parents usually because the parents forget/forgot to say the above duaa before having sex.].

HOW HE SHOULD COME TO HER.

It is allowed for a Muslim man to enter his wife in her vagina from any direction he wishes - from behind or from the front. About this Allah revealed the following verse:"Your wives are a tilth unto you; so approach your tilth when or how ye will" [al-Baqarah 223] There are also various hadith on this subject, of which I will give only 2: On the authority of Jaabir who said: "The Jews used to say that if a man entered his wife in the vagina but from behind, their child would be crosseyed! Then Allah revealed the verse: "Your wives are as a tilth unto you; so approach your tilth when or how ye will;" [al-Baqarah 223]. The Prophet said : "From the front or the back, as long as it is in the vagina". [Al-Bukhari and Muslim] On the authority of Ibn 'Abbaas who said: "The Ansaar, who had been polytheists, lived with the Jews, who were people of the book. The former viewed the latter as being superior to them in knowledge, and used to follow their example in many things. The people of the book would only make love to their wives from the side, this being the most modest way for the woman, and the Ansaar had followed their example in that. These people from the Quraish, on the other hand, used to expose their women in an uncomely manner. They took pleasure in them from the front, from the back, or laid out flat. When the Makkans came to al-Madeenah at the time of the Hijrah, one of them married a woman from among the Ansaar, and began doing that with her. She disapproved of it and told him: "We used only to be approached from the side, so do that or stay away from me!" This dispute became very serious until it reached the ears of the Prophet. So Allah, revealed the verse: "Your wives are as a tilth unto you, so approach your tilth when or how ye will;" [al-Baqarah 223] (ie. from the front, the back, or laid out flat). What is meant here is the entry which produces children." [Abu Dawood, al -Haakim and others: Hasan isnaad and is supported].

THE PROHIBITION OF SODOMY.

It is forbidden for a Muslim man to enter his wife in her anus. This is understood from the verse quoted above (i.e. since a "planting ground" can only refer to a place where something might grow), and from the narrations cited above. There are also other hadith on the subject, among them: First: On the authority of Umm Salama who said: "When the Muhajireen came to Ansaar at al-Madeenah, some of them married women from the Ansaar. The women of the Muhajireen used to lie on their faces (during intercourse), while the women of the Ansaar never did it that way. Then, one of the men of the Muhajireen wanted his wife to do that. She refused until such time as she could ask the Prophet about it. She went to the Prophet but was embarassed to ask the question, and so Umm Salama asked him. Then the verse was revealed which says: "Your wives are as a tilth unto you; so approach your tilth *when or how ye will;" [al-Baqarah 223]. The Prophet said: "No! (not any way you wish) Except in one opening! (ie. the vagina)". [Ahmad, at-Tirmidhee and others : Saheeh] Second: On the authority of Ibn 'Abbaas who said: "'Umar ibn Al-Khattaab came to the Prophet and said : 'O Messenger of Allah, I am destroyed!' The Prophet asked: 'And what has destroyed you, O 'Umar?' 'Umar said: `I turned my mount around last night.' (An expression which means he has sexual intercourse with his wife penetrating the vagina while mounting her from the rear.) The Prophet gave him no answer and when the revelation came and the verse was revealed which says: "Your wives are as a tilth unto you; so approach your tilth when or how ye will;" [al-Baqarah 223] and the Prophet said,From the front and from the back, just beware of her anus and her menses". [an-Nasaa'ee in "`Ishratun-Nisaa" with hasan isnaad, atTirmidhi and others]. Third: On the authority of Khuzaima ibn Thaabit who said: "A man asked the Prophet about entering women in the rear, or the entering by a man of his wife in her rear, and the Prohet answered: `Halaal (ie. permissible).' When the man turned to leave, the Prophet called him or ordered for him to be called back and said : "What did you say? In which of the 2 openings did you mean? If what you meant was from her rear and in her vagina, then yes. But if what you meant was from her rear and in her anus, then no. Verily Allah is not ashamed of the*

*truth - do not enter your wives in their anuses!"
[as-Shaafi, al -Baihaqi and others: Saheeh]
Fourth: "Allah does not look at one who comes
to his wife in her anus". [an-Nasaa'ee: Hasan
isnaad and supported in "al-'Ishrah"; at-
Tirmidhee and Ibn Hibbaan]. Fifth: "Cursed
are those who come to their wives in their
anuses." [Abu Dawood, Ahmad and others with
hasan isnaad and is supported]. Sixth:
"Whoever has sexual intercourse with a
mentruating woman, or a woman in her anus,
or approaches a soothsayer and believes what
he is told has disbelieved in that which was
revealed to Muhammad." [Aboo Dawood, at-
Tirmidhee and others: Saheeh].*

CHAPTER EIGHT

PERFORMING WUDHUU BEFORE THE BED INTERCOURSE.

PERFORMING WUDUU BEFORE THE BED INTERCOURSE.

When a Muslim man has had sexual intercourse with his wife in the legal manner and then wishes to return another time, he should first perform wudhuu', based on the statement of the Prophet : "When one of you comes to his wife and then wishes to return another time, let him perform wudhuu' between the 2 times (In another version, the same wudhuu' which he performs for prayer) for verily, it will invigorate his return." [Muslim, Ibn Abi Shaibah and others].

BATHING IS PREFERABLE.

Bathing, however, is preferable to merely making wudhuu' in such situations. Abu Raafi' narrates: "That the Prophet made the rounds of all his wives one night, bathing in the house of each one. He (i.e. the narrator) asked the Prophet: "Couldn't you have just bathed once (i.e. at the end)?" The Prophet answered: "This way is purer, cleaner and better". [Ab Daawood, anNasaa'ee: Hasan in "al-'Ishrah", and others].

THE BATHING OF HUSBAND AND WIFE TOGETHER.

It is permissible for the husband and wife to bath together in the same place even though he sees her private parts, and she sees his. This is established by a number of authentic hadith, among them: On the authority of 'Aa'ishah (radiallahu anha) who said: "I used to bathe with the Prophet from a single container of water which was placed between us such that our hands collideuinside it. He used to race me such that I would say: `Leave some for me, leave some for me!' She added: `We were in a state of Janaba (i.e. the state of having slept together).'" [Al-Bukhari and Muslim]. On the authority of Mu'aawiya ibn Haida, who said:

"I said: `O Messenger of Allaah, which of our nakedness is allowed, and of which must we beware?' The Prophet answered, "Guard your nakedness excpet from your wife or those whom your right hand possesses." (So it is permissible for both spouses to look at and touch the body of his or her companion even the private parts). He said: `O Messenger of Allah, what about if the relatives live together with each other?' The Prophet answered : "If you can make sure that no one ever sees your nakedness, then do so." He said: `O Messenger of Allah, what about when one is alone?' The Prophet said: "Allah is more deserving of your modesty than are the people"." [Ahmad, Abu Dawood, at-Tirmidhee and others: Saheeh].

MAKING WUDHUU AFTER SEX AND BEFORE SLEEPING.

It is best for husband and wife not to sleep after having sex until they first perform wudhuu'. There are various hadith about this, among them: First: On the authority of 'Aa'shah who said: "Whenever the Prophet wished to sleep or eat while in a state of Janaba (i.e. after having sex and before bathing), he would wash his private parts and perform wudhuu' as for prayer." [Al-Bukhaari and Muslim]. Second: On the authority of Ibn 'Umar who said: "O Messenger of Allah, should we go to sleep in a state of janaba?" The Prophet answered: "Yes, after making wudhuu." [Al- Bukhaaree and Muslim]. In another version: "Perform wudhuu' and wash your private parts, and then sleep." [Al -Bukhaaree and Muslim]. And, in another version: "Yes, you can perform wudhuu', sleep, and bathe whenever you want." [Muslim and al-Baihaqi]. And, in still another version: "Yes, and perform wudhuu' if you wish." (This last version proves that this wudhuu' is not obligatory.) [Ibn Khuzima and Ibn Hibban: Saheeh]. Third: On the authority of 'Ammaar ibn Yaasir, the Prophet said: "There are three which the angels will never approach: The corpse of a disbeliever; a man who wears perfume of women; and, one who has had sex until he performs wudhuu'." [Abu Dawood, Ahmad and others: Hasan].

THE RULING OF THIS WUDHUU.

This wudhuu' is not obligatory, but is very highly and definitely commendable. This (i.e. its not being obligatory) is based on the hadith narrated by 'Umar in which he asked the Prophet: "Should we go to sleep in a state of janaba?" To which the Prophet answered: "Yes, and perform wudhuu' if you wish." [Ibn Hibbaan: Saheeh]. This is also supported by other hadith, among them a hadith narrated by 'Aa'ishah who said: "The Prophet used to sleep in a state of janaba without having touched water, until he would get up later and bathe." [Ibn Abi Shaiba, at-Tirmidhee, Abu Daawood and others: Saheeh]. In another version narrated by 'Aa'ishah , she said: ""He used to spend the night in a state of janaba until Bilal came in the morning to make the adhaan. Then, he would get up, bathe while I looked at the water dripping from his head, and go out. Then, I would hear his voice in the Fajr prayer. Then, he would remain fasting." Mutarrif said:

"I said to Aamir: In the month of Ramadhaan?" He said: "Yes, in Ramadhaan and in other than Ramadhaan." [Ibn Abi Shaiba, Ahmad and others: Saheeh].

MAKING TAYAMMUM IN A STATE OF JANABA INSTEAD OF WUDHUU.

It is also permissible to make Tayammum sometimes instead of wudhuu' before sleeping. This is based on a hadith of 'Aa'ishah in which she said: "When the Prophet was in a state of janaba and wished to sleep, he used to make wudhuu' or Tayammum." [Al- Baihaqi: Hasan]

BATHING BEFORE SLEEPING.

Bathing however, is perferable to any of the above- mentioned possibilities as is clear in the hadith of `Abullaah ibn Qais who said: "I asked 'Ai'ishah : What did the Prophet do when in a state of janaba? Did he bathe before sleeping or sleep before bathing?" She answered: "He did all of those things. Sometimes he bathe and then slept. And sometimes he performed wudhuu' and then slept." I said: "Praise be to Allah who made things flexible." [Muslim, Ahmad and Abu `Auwaana].

THE PROHIBITION OF SEX WHEN SHE IS MENSTRUATING.

It is forbidden for a Muslim man to have sexual intercourse with his wife when she is menstruating. This is clear in the following verse of the quran:"They ask thee concerning women's courses. Say: They are a hurt and a pollution: So
keep away from women in their courses, and do not approach them until they are clean. But when they have purified themselves, ye may approach them in any manner, time, or place ordained for you by Allah. For Allah loves those who turn to Him constantly and He loves those who keep themselves pure and clean." [Al-Baqarah, 222] There are also hadith about this, among them: First: "Whoever has sexual intercourse with a menstruating woman, or a woman in her anus, or approaches a soothsayer

and believes what he is told has disbelieved in that which was revealed to Muhammad." Second: On the authority of Anas ibn Malik, who said: "When one of their women has their period, the Jews used to put her out of the house, and they would not eat, drink, or sleep with her in the house. The Prophet was asked about this, and Allah revealed the verse: "They ask thee concerning women's courses. Say: They are a hurt and a pollution: so keep away from women in their courses, ... Then the Prophet said: "Be with them in the house, and do everything except for intercourse itself." The Jews said: "This man wants to leave nothing which we do without doing something different." Then, Asyad ibn Hudair said: "O Messenger of Allah, verily the Jews says such-and-such, shoudl we not then have sexual intercourse during menstruation?" The Prophet's face changed such that they thought that he was enraged with them, so they left. As they were coming out, they saw a gift of milk being brought to the Prophet. The Prophet then sent someone after them to give them a drink of milk, so they felt that he was not actually angry with them." [Muslim, Abu 'Auwaana and Abu Daawood].

THE PENITENCE OF ONE WHO HAS SEX DURING MENSES.

Whoever is overcome by desire and has sexual intercourse with his wife when she is menstruating and before she becomes clean must give the value of one dinar's weight of gold or about 4.25 grams (4.2315 to be more precise), or half that amount. This is based on a hadith narrated by 'Abdullaah ibn 'Abbaas from the Prophet in relation to one who enters his wife while she is on her period as follows: "Let him give one dinar in charity, or one half dinar." [At-Tirmidhee, Abu Dawood, At-Tabaraani and others: Saheeh

WHAT IS PERMISSIBLE WHEN SHE IS ON HER PERIODS.

It is allowed for him to enjoy pleasure with his wife in any way except for her private parts when she is on her period. There are several hadiths about this: First: "and do everything except intercourse itself." [Muslim, Abu 'Auwaana and Abu Daawood] Second: On the authority of 'Aa'ishah who said: "When we were on our periods, the Prophet used to order us to put on a waist cloth that her husband can then lie with her." One time she said: "... her husband can then fondle and caress her." [al-Bukhaari, Muslims and others]. Third: On the authority of one of the wives of the Prophet who said: "When the Prophet wanted something from one of his wives who was on her period, he put a cloth over her private parts, and then did whatever he wanted." [Abu Daawood: Saheeh]

WHEN IS IT ALLOWED TO RESUME SEXUAL ACTIVITY AFTER MENSES?

When she becomes clean of any menstrual blood, and the flow stops completely, it is allowed for them to resume sexual activity after she washes the place where the blood had been, or performs wudhuu', or takes a complete bath. Whichever of these three alternatives she does makes it allowed for them to resume sexual activity, based on Allah's statement in the quran: "But when they have purified themselves, ye may approach them in any manner, time, or place ordained for you by Allah. For Allah loves those who turn to Him constantly and He loves those who keep themselves pure and clean." [Al-Baqarah 222] This is the position of Ibn Hazm, 'Ataa, Qatadah, al-Awzaa'ee and Daawud az-Zaahiree and of Mujaahid: as Ibn Hazm says: "All three of these are a purification - so whichever of them she uses after the cessation of her periods, then she is lawful for her husband." The same term is used to mean washing the private parts in the Aayah revealed concerning the people of Qubaa: "In it are men who love to be purified; and Allah loves those who make themselves pure." [at-Tawbah

9:108] There is nothing here in the Aayah however, or in the Sunnah, to restrict the Aayah in question to any of the three meanings - and to do so requires a further proof.

THE LAWFULNESS OF COITUS INTERRUPTUS.

(Withdrawl of the penis from the vagina at the time of ejaculation with the purpose of avoiding impregnation. This can be done only with the permission of one's wife). It is allowed for a Muslim man to practise coitus interruptus with his wife. There are several hadith about this: First: On the authority of Jaabir who said: "We were practising coitus interruptus, and the qur'an was being revealed." [al-Bukhaari and Muslim]. In another version, he said: "We used to practise coitus interruptus in the lifetime of the Prophet. This reached the Prophet, and he did not prohibit us from doing it." [Muslim, an-Nasaa'ee and at-Tirmidhee]. Second: On the authority of Abu Sa'eed al-Khudhriy, who said: "A man came to the Prophet and said: "I have a young girl (right-hand possession), and I practise coitus interruptus with her. I want that which men want, but the Jews claim that coitus interruptus is minor infanticide." The Prophet said: "The Jews have lied, the Jews have lied. If Allaah wished to create a child, you would not be able to prevent it." [An- Naasaa'ee in al-'Ishrah: Abu Dawood and others: Saheeh].

Third: On the authority of Jaabir, a man came to the Prophet and said: "I have a slave girl who serves us and waters our date trees. Sometimes I go to her, but I dislike that she should become pregnant by me". The Prophet said: "use coitus interruptus if you like, but whatever has been ordained for her will come." After some time, the man again came to the Prophet and said: "She has become pregnant!" The Prophet (peace be upon him) told him: "I told you that whatever has been ordained for her will come." [Muslim, Abu Dawood and others].

IS IT PREFERABLE NOT TO PRACTICE COITUS INTERRUPTUS?

Not practising coitus interruptus is preferable for a number of reasons: First: It is harmful for the woman, since it reduces her pleasure by cutting it short. If she agrees to it, it still contains the following negetive points. Second: It negates part of the purpose of marriage which is enlarging the Muslim nation through offspring, as in the statement of the Prophet: "Marry the loving and fertile, for I will compete with the other Prophets with the number of my followers." [Abu Dawood, an-Nasaa'ee and others: Saheeh]. This is why the Prophet once referred to it as "minor infanticide" (and not because it is forbidden as infanticide is forbidden) when asked about it saying: "That is minor infanticide". [Muslim, Ahmad and al-

Baihaqi]. For this was preferable in the hadith narrated by Abu Sa'eed al-Khudhriy saying: "Coitus Interruptus was mentioned in the presence of the Prophet and he said: "Why would one of you do that? (note he did not say "let none of you do that") Allah is the Creator of every single soul." [Muslim]. In another version, he said: "You act and you act. There are no people destined to be from now until the day of Qiyama but that all of them will be." [Muslim]

WHAT THE TWO SPOUSES SHOULD INTEND WITH THEIR MARRIAGE.

Both spouses should enter into marriage with the following intentions: freeing themselves of unfulfilled sexual desires, and protecting themselves from falling into that which Allaah has forbidden (i.e. adultery and fornication). What's more, a reward as the reward for sadaqa (voluntary giving of charity)

is recorded for them every time they have sex. This is based on the following hadith of the Prohpet narrated by Abu Dharr: "Some of the companions of the Prophet said to him: 'O Messenger of Allaah, the affluent among us have taken the rewards (of the hereafter)! They pray as we pray, fast as we fast, and then they give charity from the surplus of their wealth!" The Prophet said: "Did Allaah not make for you that from which you can give sadaqa? Verily for every time you say Subhannallah (Exalted is Allah) there is a sadaqa, and for every time you say Allahuakbar (Allah is Most Great) there is a sadaqa, and for every time you say Al-Hamdulillah (Praise is to Allah) there is sadaqa, and in every act of enjoining what is right there is sadaqa, and in every act of forbidding what is wrong there is a sadaqa,and in your sexual relations there is a sadaqa." The Companions said: "O Messenger of Allaah , is there a reward for one of us when he satisfies his sexual desire?" The Prophet said: "Don't you see, if he had satisfied it with the forbidden, would there not have been a sin upon him?" They said: "Why, yes!" He said: "In the same way, when he satisfies it with that which is lawful, there is for him in that a reward." [Muslim, an- Nasaa'ee in al-'Ishrah, and Ahamd].

WHAT HE SHOULD DO THE MORNING AFTER HIS WEDDING NIGHT.

It is desirable for the husband to go to his relatives who came to visit him in his house, on the following morning, to give them greetings and pray for them. It is also desirable for them to do likewise for him, as in the following hadith narrated by Anas : "The Messenger of Allah gave a feast on the morning of his wedding night with Zainab, at which he fed the Muslims to satisfaction on bread and meat. Then, he went out to the Mothers of the Believers (i.e. to his other wives), gave them greetings and prayed for them, which they returned in kind. This is the way he used to do on the morning after a wedding night." [Ibn Sa'd and an-Nasaa'ee: Saheeh].

THE HOUSE MUST HAVE PLACE FOR BATHING.

The married couple must have a place to bathe in their house, and the husband must not allow his wife to go to the public bath houses. This is forbidden, and here are various hadith about it, among them: First: On the authority of Jaabir who said: "The Prophet said: "Whoever believes in Allah and the Last Day, let him not allow his wife to go to the Public baths. Whoever believes in Allah and the Last Day, let him not go to the baths except with a waist-cloth. And whoever believes in Allah and the Last Day, let him never sit at a table at which intoxicants are being circulated." [Al-Haakim, at-Tirmidhee and others: Saheeh] Second: On the authority of Umm ad-Dardaa' who said: "I came out of the public bath and I met Allaah's Messenger who said to me: 'From where have you come O Umm Dardaa'?' I said: 'From the baths'. Then he said: "By the One in whose hand is my soul, every woman who removes her clothes anywhere except the house of one of her mothers has torn down all that veils her before ar-Rahman." [Ahmad : Saheeh] Third: On the authority of Abu al-Maleeh who said: "Some women from Ash-Shaam entered upon 'Aa'ishah and said : "Where are you from?" The women answered: "We are of the people of Ash-Shaam (the area of presentday Syria)." 'Aa'ishah said: "Are you perhaps from that district which allows its women to enter the public baths?" The said: "Yes". She said: "As for me, I heard the Messenger of Allaah say: "Every woman who removes her clothes other than in her house has torn down all veils of modesty between herself and Allaah." [at-Tirmidhee, Abu Dawood and others: Saheeh] .

CHAPTER NINE

PROHIBITION OF SPREADING BEDROOM SECRETS.

THE PROHIBITION OF SPREADING BEDROOM SECRETS.

It is forbidden for either the husband or the wife to spread any of the secrets of their bedroom to anyone outside. The following two hadith are about this: First: "Verily among the worst people before Allah on the Day of Judgement is a man who approaches his wife sexually and she responds and then he spreads her secrets." [Muslim, Ibn Abi Shaiba, Ahmad and others]. Second: "On the authority of Asmaa bint Yazid who narrated "that she was once in the presence of the Prophet and there were both men and wo men sitting. The Prophet then said: "Perhaps a man might discuss what he does with his wife, or perhaps a woman might inform someone what she did with her husband?" The people were silent. Then I said: "O, Yes! O Messenger of Allaah verily both the women and men do that." Then the Prophet said: "Do not do that. It is like a male shaitaan who meets a female shaitaan along the way, and has sex with her while the people look on!" [Ahmad: Hasan or Saheeh due to supports]

THE OBLIGATION OF A WEDDING FEAST.

The husband must sponsor a feast after the consummation of the marriage. This is based on the order of the Prophet to 'Abur-Rahman ibn 'Auf to do so, and on the hadith narrated by Buraida ibn At-Haseeb, who said: "When 'Ali sought the hand of Faatimah (the Prophet's daughter) in marraige, he said that the Prophet said: "A wedding (and in another version "a bridegroom") must have a feast." The narrator said: "Sa'ad said: '(a feast) of a sheep.' Someone
else said: 'Of such and such a quantity of corn."
[Ahmad and at-Tabaraani: Its isnaad is acceptable as al -Haafiz Ibn Hajr says in Fathul -Baaree: 9/188]

THE SUNNAH OF THE WEDDING FEAST.

The following should be observed with regard to the wedding banquet: First: It should be held ('aqb - Fathul Baaree: 9/242-244) three days after the first wedding night, since this is the tradition of the Prophet which has reached us. On the authority of Anas who said: "The Prophet entered upon his wife and sent me to invite some men for food." [al-Bukhaari and al-Baihaqi]. Also on the authority of Anas, he said: "The Prophet married Safiya, and her freedom was her dowry. He gave the feast for three days." [Abu Ya'laa and others: Hasan]. Second: One should invite the righteous to his banquet whether they be rich or poor. The Prophet said: "Do not be the friend of any except believers, and have only the pious eat your food." [Abu Dawood, at-Tirmidhee and others: Saheeh]. Third: If one is able, he should have a feast of one or more sheep. Based on the following hadith, Anas said: "Abdur-Rahmaan came to al-Madeenah, and the Prophet assigned Sa'ad ibn Ar-Rabee' al-Ansaariy as his brother. Sa'ad took him to his house, culled for food, and they both ate. The Sa'ad said: "O my brother, I am the wealthiest of the people of al-Madeenah (in another version: "... of the Ansaar"), so look to half of my property and take it (in another version: "... and I will divide my garden in half"). Also, I have two wives (and you, my brother in Allah, have no wife), so look to which of mine pleases you more, so I can divorce her for you. Then upon the completion of the prescribed waiting period, you may marry her." 'Abdur-Rahmaan said: "No, by Allah, may Allah bless you in your family and your property. Show me the way to the market-place."And so they showed him the way to the market-place and he went there. He bought and he sold and he made a profit. In the evening , he came back to the people of his house with some dried milk for cooking and some ghee. After that some time elapsed, until he appeared one day with traces of saffron on his garments. The Prophet said to him: "What is this?" He said: "O Messenger of Allah, I have married a woman among the Ansaar." The Prophet answered: "What did you give her for her dowry?" He answered: "The weight of five dirhams in gold." Then, the Prophet said: "May Allah bless you, give a feast if only with one sheep." 'Abdur-Rahmaan said: "I have seen myself in such a state that if I were to lift a stone, I would expect to find some gold or silver under it." Anas said: "I saw after his death that each of his wives inherited one hundred thousand Dinars." [Al-Bukhaari, an-Nasaa'ee and others]. Also on the authority of Anas he said: "I never saw the Prophet sponsor such a wedding feast as the one he gave for Zainab. He slaughtered a sheep and fed everyone meat and bread until they ate no more." [Al-Bukhaari, Muslim and others].

WEDDING FEAST WITHOUT MEAT.

It is allowed to give the wedding banquet with any food which is available and affordable, even if that does not include meat. This is based on the following hadith narrated by Anas: "The Prophet stayed between Khaibar and al-Madeenah for three days during which he had entered with his wife Safiya . Then I invited the Muslims to his Wedding feast. There was neither meat nor bread at his feast. Rather, leather eating mats were brought out and on them were placed dates, dried milk, and clarifi ed butter. The people ate their fill." [Al-Bukhaari, Muslim and others].

PARTICIPATION OF THE WEALTHY IN THE FEAST.

It is commendable for the wealthy to help in the preparations for the wedding feast based on the hadith narrated by Anas about the Prophet's marriage to Safiya: "Then, when we were on the road, Umm Sulaim prepared her (Safiya) for him (the Prophet and brought her to him at night, and so the the Prophet awoke the next morning a new bridgegroom. Then he said: "Whoever has something, let him bring it." (In another version, he said "Whoever has an excess of provisions, let him bring it.") Anas continues: "And so the leather eating mats were spread out and one man would bring dried milk, another dates and another clarified butter and so they made Hais (hais is a mixture of the above three things). The people then ate of this hais and drank from pools of rainwater which were nearby, and that was the wedding feast of the Prophet." [Al-Bukhaari, Muslims and others].